A BUSINESS APPROACH TO POTATO FARMING

Complete Entrepreneurial Step By Step Guide To Potato Garden From Scratch

ZHURI HART

DISCLAIMER

This book is intended to provide general information and insights on adopting a business approach to farming. The content within is based on the author's knowledge and experiences up to the date of publication. It is essential to recognize that the field of agriculture is dynamic, influenced by various factors such as market conditions, climate, and regulatory changes.

Readers are advised to conduct thorough research, seek professional advice, and consider their unique circumstances before implementing any strategies or practices discussed in this book. The author and publisher disclaim any responsibility for the accuracy, completeness, or suitability of the information provided. The book is not a substitute for professional advice, and the author and publisher shall not be liable for any damages or losses arising from the use or reliance on the information presented herein.

Individual results may vary, and success in farming enterprises is contingent upon numerous variables. The author encourages readers to consult with relevant experts, agricultural extension services, and legal or financial professionals to tailor strategies to their specific needs and local conditions.

This book is not intended to be a comprehensive guide to all aspects of farming, and readers should exercise their judgment and discretion in applying the principles discussed. The author and publisher do not endorse any specific products, services, or companies mentioned in this book unless explicitly stated.

By reading this book, the reader acknowledges and accepts the inherent uncertainties in agricultural endeavors and agrees to use the information at their own risk.

TABLE OF CONTENTS

ABOUT THE BOOK

"A Business Approach to Potato Farming," a book, offers a thorough manual for anyone wishing to get into the potato farming business or improve their current operations. The book offers insightful information on all aspects of potato farming, from market dynamics to sustainable practices and technology integration, with a strong emphasis on business principles.

The book establishes the scene in the first section by exploring the history of potato farming and describing the particular goals it seeks to accomplish. It provides an answer to the basic query of why potato farming exists, highlighting the importance of potatoes in world agriculture. This foundational work provides readers with a logical development by setting the stage.

The book provides a broad overview of the market before delving deeply into the potato sector. By highlighting current issues and trends, it puts readers in a position to make wise choices. The chapter goes on to emphasize farming potential related to potatoes, providing a foundation for business owners looking to profit from an important and adaptable commodity.

Readers are taken through the first steps of starting a potato farm. From choosing the best potato types to comprehending soil and climate issues, this book offers helpful guidance on the crucial elements impacting a prosperous beginning. It also covers crucial elements like infrastructure and equipment, guaranteeing a comprehensive strategy for establishing a sustainable potato-growing business.

The book presents the key elements of business planning for a potato farm. It focuses on financial estimates, risk management techniques, market research, and the fundamentals of company planning. By giving readers the resources they need to build a solid business foundation, this section will help them match their potato farming aspirations with long-term success.

The technical components of potato farming are covered in detail, including crop care and planting, irrigation techniques, managing pests and diseases, and using sustainable and organic farming methods. These chapters address the growing demand for sustainable and organic produce by offering a thorough manual for maximizing agricultural productivity while reducing environmental effects.

The relationship between technology and potato farming is examined. Topics covered include automation, data analytics, mechanization, and precision farming.

Through the integration of technology, the book enables readers to remain up to date with industry developments, thereby augmenting efficiency and production.

The book concentrates on potato marketing and sales, with a particular emphasis on customer relationship development, distribution methods, export potential, and brand creation. To ensure that readers are knowledgeable about agricultural regulations, environmental compliance, safety, and health standards, it discusses the crucial topic of regulations and compliance.

"A Business Approach to Potato Farming" is a priceless tool for anyone wishing to navigate the potato farming sector. It serves novice and seasoned farmers alike who want to improve their operations in this vital and ever-changing field by fusing pragmatism with a strategic business strategy.

CHAPTER ONE

POTATO FARMING INTRODUCTION

KNOWING THE POTATO INDUSTRY

The potato industry is a vital part of the global agricultural economy that is responsible for feeding a wide range of populations across the globe. A thorough understanding of the potato sector necessitates exploring a range of topics, such as market dynamics, stakeholder concerns, and cultivation practices. The purpose of this overview is to shed light on the major factors that influence the potato sector, including the overall landscape of the potato market, current trends, obstacles, and possible prospects associated with potato farming.

AN OVERVIEW OF THE MARKET FOR POTATOES

The market for potatoes is notable for its enormous size and importance in both industrialized and developing nations. As a staple food in many cultures, potatoes provide millions of people with essential calories and nourishment. The potato industry's market dynamics are shaped by various variables, including worldwide commerce, agricultural methods, consumer demand, and technical improvements. The market is complicated by the wide range of potato varieties, different processing techniques, and the adaptability of the produce.

PRESENT PATTERNS AND OBSTACLES

Understanding the dominant trends and obstacles that influence the potato industry's future course is crucial for managing it. Advances in technology, such as biotechnology and precision agriculture, have an impact on farming methods. Potato production is also challenged by shifting customer choices, environmental concerns, and the effects of climate change. To further highlight the industry's many challenges, sustainable practices, effective supply chain management, and resolving food security issues are vital.

POSSIBILITIES FOR GROWING POTATOES

Notwithstanding the difficulties, there are important prospects in potato cultivation that should be investigated. Potato growing can become more sustainable and efficient with the help of farming innovations like precision farming and vertical farming. Furthermore, markets for environmentally concerned potato producers are opened by the growing demand for locally grown and organic goods. There are opportunities for revenue development by diversifying into value-added items such as processed potato products and specialty types.

A thorough analysis of the market, knowledge of current trends, and a proactive attitude to problem-solving are all necessary for a sophisticated grasp of the potato sector. In addition to overcoming current obstacles, stakeholders may enhance the industry's resilience and sustainability in the face of a changing agricultural landscape by realizing the opportunities presented by potato farming.

CHAPTER TWO

HOW TO BEGIN USING POTATO

CHOOSING THE CORRECT TYPES OF POTATOES

Selecting the right potato types is essential to a profitable potato-growing endeavor. Varieties differ in terms of yield, resistance to disease, and climate adaptability. It's critical to take into account elements like the potatoes' intended use, consumer demand, and the unique growing circumstances in the area.

Popular potato cultivars include Russet, Yukon Gold, and Kennebec, each with distinctive qualities to suit a range of tastes and culinary requirements. To ascertain which cultivars are most appropriate for their particular farming objectives and environmental circumstances, farmers should carry out in-depth research and speak with local agricultural extension services.

CROP ROTATION AND SOIL PREPARATION

A key component of potato farming that directly affects crop health and productivity is soil preparation. Loose, nutrient-rich soils that drain well are ideal for potato growth. Farmers should test their soil to determine its pH and nutrient levels, then apply the appropriate amendments to correct any shortages.

To prepare the soil adequately, a suitable seedbed must be created by harrowing and plowing. To reduce the risk of pests and diseases that target potatoes specifically, crop rotation is also essential. Potato crops should be alternated with unrelated crops to disrupt disease cycles and enhance soil health in general.

Long-term production can be increased by using sustainable techniques like cover crops, which can further improve soil fertility and structure.

CLIMATE AND ENVIRONMENTAL FACTORS TO TAKE INTO ACCOUNT

Because potatoes are temperature-sensitive, selecting varieties that are appropriate for the area's climate is essential to successful farming. During the growing season, potatoes typically prefer cool areas with temperatures between 60 and 70°F (15 and 21°C). Potato plants should be planted during periods of favorable weather since frost might harm them. Potatoes need steady moisture throughout their growth cycle, especially during tuber development, therefore adequate water management is crucial. Because some climatic conditions can encourage the spread of potato illnesses and draw pests, environmental considerations also include disease prevention and pest control.

A healthy crop requires constant observation and integrated pest management techniques.

INFRASTRUCTURE AND EQUIPMENT

The secret to maximizing potato farming operations is to make the appropriate infrastructural and equipment investments. Planters, harvesters, and storage facilities are examples of planting and harvesting equipment that is essential for maintaining productivity and lowering labor expenses. When purchasing equipment, farmers should carefully consider their unique requirements as well as their financial limits. For a steady supply of water, proper irrigation systems—such as sprinklers or drip irrigation—are necessary. Harvested potatoes should have an extended shelf life by being stored in environments that are ideal for preventing sprouting and spoiling. Transportation access is another aspect of an adequate infrastructure that enables prompt delivery to markets. Maintaining a productive and successful potato farming business requires routine infrastructure and equipment upgrades and maintenance.

CHAPTER THREE

ORGANIZING YOUR POTATO FARM ENTERPRISE

ESSENTIALS OF BUSINESS PREPARATION

To achieve long-term success, starting a potato farm business involves meticulous preparation. Start by describing your company's objectives, vision, and mission. Define your target market and the special value that your potato farm offers to clients. Make sure to develop a strong organizational structure and identify important partners and stakeholders. A thorough business strategy will act as your road map as you negotiate the potential and difficulties present in the potato growing sector.

MARKET ANALYSIS AND RESEARCH

Finding possible agricultural niches and comprehending the workings of the potato industry require extensive market research. Examine market trends, consumer preferences, and the competitive environment. Determine which potato types are in demand and look into possible distribution routes. Gaining a competitive edge in the market by customizing your potato farming business to satisfy customer expectations depends on your understanding of the needs and preferences of the market.

FINANCIAL PROJECTIONS AND BUDGETING

Make a thorough budget that lists all of the expenses related to establishing and operating your potato farm. Take into account costs for labor, marketing, seeds, fertilizer, equipment, and land purchase. Create accurate financial estimates that take into consideration any changes in crop yields, potato prices, and other market factors.

In addition to helping you obtain funding, a well-organized budget will act as a financial roadmap to direct your expenditure and guarantee long-term profitability.

RISK MANAGEMENT TECHNIQUES

Weather variations, pest infestations, and market volatility are among the inherent hazards associated with potato cultivation, much like any other agricultural endeavor. Create effective risk management plans to lessen these difficulties. Increase crop variety diversity to reduce the impact of individual risks. Invest in insurance to guard against unanticipated events causing crop loss. To proactively modify your plans, stay up to date on market conditions and industry changes. Your potato farm will remain sustainable over time if you incorporate resilience into your business plan to help you deal with adversity.

Careful market research, a well-considered budget, and efficient risk management techniques are essential components of successful potato farm business planning. By taking care of these important ideas, you'll be in a better position to start and maintain a successful potato farming business.

CHAPTER FOUR

POTATO FARMING METHODS

HANDLING CROPS AND PLANTING

Choosing healthy seed potatoes is the first step in the potato cultivation process. These tubers have good sprouting eyes and are devoid of infections. To ensure a good crop, farmers should make sure the seed potatoes are verified. Potatoes are normally grown in hills or rows, and planting takes place in the spring. To provide plants enough room to grow and to promote air circulation, which lowers the risk of disease, proper spacing is essential.

Potato plants must be regularly observed as part of crop care. A typical technique called "hilling" involves mounding dirt around the base of plants to shield budding tubers from sunlight and keep them from becoming green. To lessen competition for nutrients and stop the development of disease, weeding is crucial.

During the growing season, farmers also need to be on the lookout for symptoms of diseases and pests.

TECHNIQUES FOR IRRIGATION

For the whole growth season, potatoes need constant hydration. Depending on the environment and available resources, a variety of irrigation techniques can be used. Water waste is reduced with drip irrigation, an effective technique that provides water straight to the roots. To control water flow, furrow irrigation entails forming canals between rows. Another method is sprinkler watering, which covers the entire area uniformly.

When to water is very important. Potatoes are susceptible to situations that are wet or dry. Sustaining soil moisture at a constant level is critical for yield optimization, particularly during critical growth stages like tuber formation. Irrigation management done correctly also helps ward off diseases that thrive in environments that are too wet or too dry.

MANAGEMENT OF PESTS AND DISEASES

An efficient management of pests and diseases is essential to a good potato crop. Aphids, nematodes, and potato beetles are common pests. Three methods of managing pests are crop rotation, using resistant potato types, and introducing helpful insects. It is crucial to regularly inspect fields to find early indications of infestations.

If left unchecked, diseases like early and late blight can destroy potato harvests. Farmers can use fungicides preventively, but to guarantee their efficacy, they must follow suggested application schedules.

Disease prevention is aided by cultural customs like timely harvesting, hilling, and appropriate spacing. Biological, cultural, and chemical techniques are combined in integrated pest management (IPM) strategies to provide a comprehensive approach to disease and pest control.

GATHERING AND KEEPING IN STORE

When the potato plants are mature and the foliage starts to wither back, harvesting usually takes place. Digging carefully is essential to prevent damage to the tubers. After harvesting, potatoes are typically cured to harden their skins and promote healing of any damage. In addition to extending storage life, proper curing lowers the risk of illness.

To stop sprouting and rot, storage facilities need to offer the best possible conditions. Cool, dark, and well-ventilated areas are the ideal places to store potatoes. Controlling humidity levels is important since too much moisture might cause spoiling. Throughout the storage period, it is crucial to regularly check for indications of sprouting, rot, or pest infestation. Good harvesting and storing techniques provide potatoes with a longer shelf life and preserve their quality for market distribution.

CHAPTER FIVE

ORGANIC AND SUSTAINABLE POTATO FARMING METHODS

ORGANIC CERTIFICATION

Getting organic certification is a crucial factor that sets organic and sustainable potato growing practices apart from traditional ones. When a potato is certified organic, it means that it was grown under stringent guidelines that forbid the use of artificial pesticides, herbicides, and genetically modified organisms (GMOs). Potatoes grown by farmers who maintain organic certification are grown using natural and sustainable methods, which promotes ecologically responsible and friendly activities.

This certification increases consumer confidence in the quality and authenticity of the organic potatoes while also serving as evidence of the farm's dedication to sustainable agriculture.

ECO-FRIENDLY PEST MANAGEMENT

Using environmentally friendly pest management techniques is one of the main tenets of sustainable potato cultivation. Organic potato farming prioritizes the use of natural predators, crop rotation, and companion planting to control pest populations, in contrast to conventional farming, which mostly uses chemical pesticides. Predatory beetles and ladybugs are examples of beneficial insects that can be introduced to help reduce pests without endangering the ecology. The use of integrated pest management (IPM) techniques emphasizes a comprehensive strategy that reduces environmental impact while preserving efficient insect control. This methodology not only preserves consumer health but also enhances the agricultural landscape's overall biodiversity.

CONSERVATION AND SOIL HEALTH

Organic and sustainable potato growing methods place a high priority on maintaining healthy soil. Farmers understand that minimal soil disturbance, cover crops, and organic amendments are key to preserving and improving soil fertility. Organic potato farming relies on compost, manure, and green manure to naturally enrich the soil instead of artificial fertilizers and chemical inputs. One essential strategy to stop soil erosion and improve nutrient cycling is crop rotation. By implementing these techniques, organic potato farming helps to preserve soil by reducing erosion and encouraging water retention in the soil. In addition to supporting strong potato crops, healthy soils are essential for sequestering carbon, which helps slow down global warming.

SUSTAINABLE AGRICULTURAL PRACTICES

In potato farming, sustainability refers to a wider range of agricultural practices rather than just certain production techniques. Sustainable agriculture aims to achieve a balance between meeting the requirements of the present without sacrificing the ability of future generations to meet their own needs.

It does this by integrating environmental, social, and economic issues. This strategy calls for maximizing the use of available resources, encouraging biodiversity, and implementing eco-friendly behaviors. This encompasses ethical labor practices, appropriate energy use, and effective water management in the context of sustainable potato farming. A dedication to resilience and long-term viability, acknowledging the interdependence of ecosystems and the significance of protecting natural resources for the benefit of farmers and the larger community, is what it means to embrace sustainability in agriculture.

Sustainable agricultural techniques, eco-friendly pest management, soil health and conservation, and organic certification serve as the cornerstones of ethical and ecologically conscious potato production. Farmers that follow these guidelines not only grow potatoes that are healthier and more nutrient-dense, but they also improve society and the environment as a whole.

CHAPTER SIX

TECHNOLOGY AND POTATO FARMING

ACCURATE FARMING

Precision farming, sometimes referred to as precision agriculture, is a cutting-edge farming methodology that leverages technology to maximize crop yields, minimize waste, and improve overall agricultural practices' efficiency. Precision farming in the context of potato farming refers to the careful management of resources including pesticides, fertilizers, and water.

Numerous technologies, including drones, sensors, and GPS-guided tractors, are used to do this. Inputs may be applied precisely and fields can be precisely mapped by farmers, guaranteeing that resources are used effectively and strategically. By using fewer inputs than necessary, this method reduces its negative effects on the environment while simultaneously increasing production.

MACHINES AND AUTOMATION

Traditional agricultural processes have been revolutionized by automation, which has become a fundamental aspect of modern potato production. To boost production, decrease labor requirements, and streamline activities, a variety of automated systems and technology have been devised.

Automated planting and harvesting machinery is essential for potato production. Potato seeds can be planted with precision at ideal intervals by using planting technology, which guarantees consistent development and maximizes production. Cutting-edge technologies in harvesting machines allow them to efficiently dig up potatoes, sort them, and even carry out quality control activities.

Automating processes not only increases productivity but also solves the problems caused by a lack of workers, especially during busy times of the year.

ANALYTICS USING DATA IN POTATO FARMING

In potato farming, data analytics has shown to be a potent instrument for streamlining decision-making procedures. Farmers can obtain important insights about crop health, environmental conditions, and overall farm performance by gathering and evaluating data from a variety of sources, such as sensors, satellites, and on-farm machinery. Making more educated decisions about fertilizer, irrigation, and pest management is made possible by this information. Predictive modeling, which is made possible by advanced analytics, aids farmers in foreseeing future difficulties and refining their approaches to disease control and production enhancement. By optimizing resource efficiency, the use of data analytics in potato farming increases accuracy, minimizes waste, and supports sustainable farming methods. The adoption of data analytics also aids farmers in anticipating possible problems, which eventually results in higher profitability and long-term sustainability.

CHAPTER SEVEN

HOW TO PROMOTE AND SELL YOUR POTATOES

DEVELOPING YOUR POTATO BRAND

Producing high-quality potatoes is not the only step in building a successful potato brand. To set your potatoes apart from the competition, you need to take a calculated risk. Determine your USPs first, such as flavor, nutritional content or environmentally friendly agricultural methods. Create a brand name and logo that embodies these attributes and is both memorable and eye-catching.

Having a unified brand identity throughout marketing collateral, packaging and your website will help build brand recognition. To emotionally connect with customers, try informing them about your farm, your commitment to quality, and the path your potatoes take from the field to the table. Developing your brand's credibility and trust can help you succeed over the long run in the cutthroat potato industry.

CHANNELS OF DISTRIBUTION

Selecting the appropriate channels for distribution is essential to getting your potatoes in front of customers. Consider selling directly to nearby grocery stores, and farmers' markets, or forming alliances with food processors and restaurants, among other choices. Additionally, to reach a larger audience, investigate online sales platforms. While working together with distributors and wholesalers might help you reach a wider audience, it's crucial to have oversight on the processing and quality of your potatoes through the supply chain. Developing connections with important figures in the distribution network guarantees a consistent and dependable supply of your goods to the market. Evaluate each distribution channel's performance regularly, and modify your plan in response to consumer preferences and market developments.

EXPORT POSSIBILITIES

Examining export prospects can greatly expand the market that your potatoes can reach. Investigate foreign markets to determine market demand and comprehend legal specifications. Forming alliances with distributors or export agents in the intended markets can expedite the procedure and offer insightful information about local tastes and market dynamics. Make sure your potatoes adhere to all applicable legislation and fulfill international quality requirements.

Creating a solid export plan requires taking into account elements that address the unique requirements of the target market, such as packaging, pricing, and logistics of shipment. Engaging in global trade shows and fostering connections with prospective foreign purchasers can lead to profitable export prospects and foster the expansion of your potato company.

BUILDING RELATIONSHIPS WITH CUSTOMERS

A crucial component of potato marketing and sales is cultivating a strong customer base. Prioritize delivering top-notch customer service, answering questions right away, and taking care of any problems or concerns. Communicate with your clients via a variety of platforms, such as newsletters, social media, and loyalty schemes. Encourage client input and take advantage of it to keep your goods and services getting better. Creating a community around your brand can encourage recurring purchases and brand loyalty. Think about planning activities or campaigns that let consumers interact with your farm and form a bond with your company. In addition to improving customer happiness, a personalized approach to customer relationships fosters the development of brand supporters who can have a favorable impact on other competitors.

CHAPTER EIGHT

RULES AND ADHERENCE

COMPREHENDING AGRICULTURAL REGULATIONS

The techniques and procedures that are followed in the agriculture industry are mostly regulated by agricultural regulations. These rules are intended to preserve community well-being, safeguard the environment, and guarantee the safety of food products. They include a broad spectrum of topics, such as the welfare of animals, pesticide use, land use, and water management. To operate lawfully and responsibly, farmers and agribusinesses must abide by these standards.

Land use planning, which attempts to strike a balance between the demands of agricultural activity and environmental conservation, is a crucial component of agricultural legislation. For example, zoning laws define regions for agricultural use, limiting conflicts with urban expansion and restricting encroachment on protected grounds. To ensure the long-term sustainability of agricultural activities, these regulations also address matters such as soil protection, erosion control, and sustainable land management techniques.

Another essential element of agricultural legislation is water management, particularly in areas where there is a water shortage or environmental damage. Regulations frequently specify the best methods for irrigation, efficient water use, and source protection. Ensuring sustainable water management practices and reducing the environmental impact of agriculture on water resources are two benefits of compliance.

Regulations governing the use of chemicals and pesticides are intended to protect the environment and the general public's health. Farmers are required to follow regulations controlling the use of fertilizers, herbicides, and pesticides to reduce their negative effects on ecosystems and avoid contaminating water supplies.

To stay in compliance with these requirements, chemical usage usually needs to be regularly monitored and reported.

Agriculture regulations give a lot of consideration to the welfare of livestock. To guarantee the humane treatment of animals, standards are set for things like housing, transportation, and medical care. In addition to being morally right, following these rules helps ensure that safe, superior agricultural goods are produced.

ADHERENCE TO ENVIRONMENTAL STANDARDS

Adherence to rules and guidelines designed to safeguard and maintain the environment is referred to as environmental compliance. These rules address a wide range of topics, such as waste management, biodiversity preservation, and the quality of the air and water. Companies and sectors in a variety of industries, including manufacturing, energy, and agriculture, must abide by these rules to reduce their environmental impact and promote sustainable development.

To guarantee that their operations have the least possible negative impact on the ecosystem, industries frequently need to obtain licenses that specify the terms and limitations of their operations to comply with environmental regulations.

Restrictions on emissions, wastewater discharges, and waste disposal techniques may be part of these permits. It is usually required to conduct regular monitoring and reporting to ensure that the environmental standards are being followed.

Regulations governing air quality are essential for reducing the negative effects of industrial activity on the atmosphere. Pollutant emissions from industries, including sulfur dioxide, nitrogen oxides, and particulate matter, must be monitored and controlled. Installation of pollution control equipment, regular emission testing, and respect for emission limitations established by regulatory bodies are examples of compliance measures.

The main goal of water quality laws is to stop industrial discharges from contaminating water sources. Preserving water bodies from pollution, managing storm water, and treating wastewater before release are all components of compliance. Regulations about pesticide use near water sources, runoff from fields, and the preservation of aquatic ecosystems are specifically focused on agricultural activities.

The purpose of waste management legislation is to reduce the amount of hazardous waste produced and to encourage the appropriate disposal of non-hazardous trash. To protect the environment, industries must abide by regulations for trash minimization, recycling, and safe disposal. Creating planning for waste management and putting resource conservation first are common requirements of compliance.

Regulations about biodiversity protection seek to prevent negative effects on ecosystems and endangered species. Businesses might have to carry out environmental impact studies to determine how their operations might affect the local flora and fauna. It may be necessary to impose mitigation measures, like habitat restoration or preservation, to guarantee adherence to biodiversity protection objectives.

STANDARDS FOR HEALTH AND SAFETY

Standards for health and safety are essential parts of legal frameworks in many different businesses, protecting the public and employees. These regulations are especially important in industries like manufacturing, construction, and agriculture where there are many workplace dangers. In addition to being required by law, adherence to safety and health rules is crucial for creating a safe workplace and averting mishaps and injuries.

Safety regulations in the agriculture industry cover a variety of topics, such as using machinery, managing chemicals, and maintaining the infrastructure of the entire farm. Farmers must put safety precautions in place to shield employees from heavy machinery risks, like those posed by tractors and harvesters. Safety signage, PPE, and training programs are frequently used instruments to improve adherence to these regulations.

Safety regulations in the construction sector cover a broad range of tasks, including electrical work, excavation, and scaffolding. To reduce the danger of accidents and injuries, regulations prescribe the usage of protective gear, fall prevention techniques, and appropriate equipment maintenance. To guarantee awareness and adherence to safety procedures, compliance frequently entails routine inspections and employee training programs.

Safety regulations covering worker ergonomics, chemical exposure, and machinery operation apply to manufacturing plants. Installation of safety guards on machinery, appropriate ventilation systems to reduce exposure to hazardous materials, and ergonomic workplace design are a few examples of compliance measures. In manufacturing settings, compliance is maintained through routine safety audits and personnel training.

Standards for occupational health and safety cover more than just physical risks; they also take into account things like stress at work, mental health, and ergonomics. Companies are realizing more and more how important it is to foster a work climate that supports mental health and resolves stress-inducing elements. In this case, compliance means putting in place procedures and policies that promote workers' general well-being.

Sustainable and ethical business operations necessitate knowledge of and adherence to environmental compliance requirements, safety and health standards, and agricultural legislation.

www.ingramcontent.com/pod-product-compliance
Lightning Source LLC
Chambersburg PA
CBHW070839290526
45795CB00002B/923